KV-374-629

Adelaide & Northern Territory Travel Guide

Attractions, Eating, Drinking, Shopping & Places To Stay

Brenda Armitage

Copyright © 2014, Astute Press
All Rights Reserved

000000734429

DUDLEY LIBRARIES	
000000734429	
Askews & Holts	16-Oct-2014
	£5.95
ST	

No part of this publication may be reproduced, stored in a retrieval system, or transmitted, in any form or by any means without the prior written permission of the publisher, nor be otherwise circulated in any form of binding or cover other than that in which it is published and without similar condition being imposed on the subsequent purchaser.

If there are any errors or omissions in copyright acknowledgements the publisher will be pleased to insert the appropriate acknowledgement in any subsequent printing of this publication.

Although we have taken all reasonable care in researching this book we make no warranty about the accuracy or completeness of its content and disclaim all liability arising from its use

Table of Contents

Adelaide

Named by Lonely Planet as one of its 'Top 10 Must-Visit Cities of 2014', the city of Adelaide is an emerging international tourist destination in South Australia. Adelaide has also been ranked as the most liveable city in Australia and as one of the 'Top 10 Most Liveable Cities in the World' by The Economist.

From the rolling Adelaide Hills to the stunning beaches, from the heritage-listed buildings to the wide streets lined with skyscrapers, Adelaide encapsulates a complete experience for every visitor.

Located on the south east coast of Australia, Adelaide is the capital of the state of South Australia and is one of the major cities in the country. Founded in 1836, the city was the planned capital for the British province in Australia. It was intended for free settlers and was never a convict settlement like the other major Australian cities. It was named after Princess Adelaide of Saxe-Meiningen, Queen Consort to King William IV. Once called the City Of Churches for the religious freedom and civil liberties.

Cradled amidst some of the best wine regions of the country (Adelaide was the first Australian city to export wine in 1845), Adelaide is set in a systematic grid layout interspaced by public squares and parklands. There are plenty of attractions in and around the city. From the airport and the hills to the beautiful beaches, everything is just a short drive away, earning the city the moniker – The 20-minute City! It is also a popular festival city in the country with numerous annual festivals, exhibitions, and events keeping the cultural calendar chock-a-block.

A trip to Adelaide is unlike visiting any other city. The genuine warmth of the Adelaideans makes one feel welcome from the very onset. The city has many historic, scenic, and natural landmarks which are a delight to pick from during the vacation. Neighbouring attractions like the Kangaroo Island and the McVale Wine Region are great for a day trip with the whole family. One is certainly spoilt for choice in this city with such a variety of offerings. As is correctly said about Adelaide – it is waiting to be uncorked and sampled!

Culture

Being a Commonwealth city, Adelaide has had a strong British influence from its founding days. In the decades that followed, because of the liberal religious following of the city, immigrants from other European countries settled in, especially the religious non-conformists.

Post World War II saw a major influx of European immigrants followed by the Indo-Chinese in the 1970s. This diversity in ethnicity, from the Aboriginal history to the post-War migration, helped shape a unique mix of events and festivals in the city.

Even the religious monuments like the Adelaide Mosque (Little Gilbert Street), or the St Peter's Cathedral (Pennington Terrace) and the West Terrace Cemetery are an architectural delight. Festivals like the Italian Carnevale, Greek Glendi, or the German Schutzenfest bring different parts of the world under the Adelaidean sky.

There are a number of Aboriginal attractions in Adelaide. The Tandanya is the oldest Aboriginal owned multi-arts centre in the country. Free entry and free tours are available at this centre that not only displays Aboriginal art, but also hosts musical performances every week. Plaques, memorials, and artwork dedicated to the Aboriginal people can be seen at Elder Park, Adelaide Festival Centre, and Piltawodli Park.

Adelaide has many festivals throughout the year, especially in March – known as Mad March for the number of festivities. Adelaide Festival, WOMADelaide, Adelaide Casino Cup, Adelaide Cabaret Festival, and Adelaide Film Festival are just some of the events that are held in March. The winter months that follow celebrate the Come Out Festival, the LGBT Feast Festival, and the Adelaide International Guitar Festival. The Adelaide Christmas pageant, staged in early November is the largest of its kind in the world, and is attended by near half a million people.

Music lovers can choose from the formal classical opera performances to the youthful and wild pop concerts. The Town Hall and the Elder Hall hosts performances by the Adelaide Symphony Orchestra and the Adelaide Youth Orchestra. Popular concert venues include the Apollo Stadium, Adelaide Entertainment Centre, and the Adelaide Oval.

There is a lot to cheer for art lovers. Along with public art exhibits, the city has a number of art galleries including the Art Gallery of SA, BMG Art, Nexus, and the Australian Experimental Art Foundation.

Location & Orientation

Located to the north of the Fleurieu Peninsula, Adelaide is a coastal city on the Gulf of St Vincent. The closest major cities are Melbourne (653 km) and Canberra (958 km). It is served by the Adelaide International Airport (IATA: ADL) - http://www.adelaideairport.com.au/. Located about 7 km west of the Adelaide city centre, this busy airport caters to over 7 million passengers annually connecting the city to its Australian neighbours and many other cities worldwide. The airport is ranked as the 2nd best airport in the world in the 5-15 million passengers category.

There are multiple modes of transport from the airport to the city and the suburbs. The Adelaide Airport Flyer – http://www.adelaideairportflyer.com/ operates door-to-door minibus shuttles.

The public bus service, by JetBus, has connections (J1 and J2) that run every 15 minutes for the 20-miniute commute to the city centre. Single-trip ticket costs $5 (Australian dollar). Skylink Shuttle connects the airport, Keswick Interstate Rail Terminal, and the city and costs $10 ($4 to the train terminal) for the one-way trip. Taxis are readily available and are the quickest mode of transport and are often a better choice than the shuttle if there are 2 or 3 passengers. Fare to the city centre costs approximately $15; there is an extra $2 levy for all airport pickups. Rental car desks are located at the ground level and one can choose from any of the major brands including Hertz, Europcar, Avis, and Budget.

The Great Southern Railway - http://www.greatsouthernrail.com.au connects Adelaide by rail to the other Australian cities. Due to the long distances between the major Australian cities, many of the train journeys in this country are quite long but not necessarily tedious because of the stunning landscape. The Ghan connecting Adelaide to Darwin, and the India Pacific, connecting the city to Perth and Sydney are considered 2 of the greatest train journeys in the world. Fares are certainly not cheap for this lifetime experience. One-way trip from Adelaide to Darwin on The Ghan can cost from $647 (day-night seat) to $6000 (premium Gold cabin for 2 guests), whereas an Adelaide-Sydney one-way trip on the India Pacific ranges from $375 to $2400! Such is the luxury of these train rides that one can even take the car on the train!

For those opting for a cheaper alternative can choose the bus. Greyhound Australia- http://www.greyhound.com.au/ has multiple connections to the city and offers many packages as well as hop-on-hop-off passes.

Once in the city, one can use the free CityLoop buses. These buses run in a clockwise and anti-clockwise direction and connect most of the major attractions (Bus No. 99C covers a number of tourist attractions). Service is reduced after 6:00 pm and stops at midnight.

The Adelaide Metro - http://www.adelaidemetro.com.au/ is the official operator for the city tram, bus, and subway. A single trip costs $4.90 so it is always better to buy a day ticket for $9.10 for unlimited travel. Tickets can be bought on board or from corner stores and vending machines at different locations in the city. Visitors can also use the Shuttle Tram – a free service between South Terrace and North Terrace. Adelaide is also home to the Tindo – the first solar-powered bus in the world. Again a free service, the Tindo travels between North Adelaide and the city centre.

For those opting for a private vehicle, taxis are available just a call away at Access Cabs (Tel: 1300 360 940) and Suburban Taxis (Tel: 13 10 08). Rental cars are offered by all major brands. For those planning to drive, it has to be kept in mind that Australia has a left-lane driving rule. Speed limits are 110 km per hr for highways and 50 km per hr for built-up areas. Speed limits are strictly enforced and driving even 5 km above the speed limit will incur a fine. To drive in Australia, one must be 21 years of age and have an International Driver's License in English.

Cycling enthusiasts can pick a free bicycle from any of the 3 Adelaide City Bike depots near the city centre. Protective gear and a lock are given as add-on benefits. With flat streets and a visitor-friendly layout in and around the city, cycling and walking are very reasonable options to see this city.

Climate & When to Visit

Adelaide experiences a warm Mediterranean climate with mild and wet winters and warm drier summers. Being in the southern hemisphere, Adelaide has its winter between May and October when the Celsius averages a high of 17 degrees and reaches a low of around 7 degrees. June is often the coldest and the wettest month of the year. Summer months, between November and April have an average high of around 28 degrees Celsius and an average low of around 17 degrees Celsius. Due to the warm and dry weather, the Adelaide summer is the perfect time to visit the city. Many festivals and public events are also scheduled during this time of the year

Sightseeing Highlights

Adelaide Hills

Part of the Mount Lofty Ranges, the Adelaide Hills are on the east of the city of Adelaide stretching from Barossa in the north to the Kuitpo Forest in the south. It is located about a 30-minite drive from the Adelaide CBD. It can be easily reached by bus - http://www.transitplus.com.au - from the central bus station on Franklin Street. For those preferring to drive, it is recommended to download a map as there is poor signage on the hills.

Once on the Adelaide Hills, there are a number of attractions to choose from.

Mt Lofty

The highest point of the hills is the Mt Lofty at 712m above sea level. The Mt Lofty Lookout - http://www.mtloftysummit.com/ is a must-visit place on the hills with stunning panoramic views of the city and the Gulf of St Vincent. The restaurant and the café at the lookout is the ideal place for a drink or a romantic dinner with the sunset as the backdrop. Reservations are strongly recommended for those who are planning a dinner at the restaurant. There is also a plaza where many private and public events are hosted.

Botanic Gardens of Adelaide – Mt Lofty

Located on the hills with stunning views, the Botanic Garden (Tel: 08 8370 8370) has collections from various parts of the world including South America, North America, East Africa, New Zealand, China, and South East Asia. Spanning over 100 hectares, it has an expansive bushland, artistic sculptures, and many walking and hiking trails. It is open from 8:30 am to 4:00 pm on weekdays and from 10:00 am to 5:00 pm on weekends, but may remain closed if there is any prediction of fire danger. Admission is free.

Hahndorf

The small town of Hahndorf is the oldest surviving German settlement in Australia. A centre for farming in the past, the town is currently dependant on the tourism industry.

The German influence and heritage is still retained in Hahndorf as one can see many German bakeries and goods outlets. In fact, one will find many boutique cellars on the main street, giving a very European feel to the town. Walking along the main street, one is also greeted by century old elm trees and beautifully restored buildings.

2 of the religious attractions in town are the 1839 St Michael's Lutheran Church - the oldest Lutheran church in Australia; and the 1846 St Lutheran Church. The cold-climate of the town is ideal for winemaking and there are many opportunities to try the local wine which has made a name for itself in the global market. If visiting during the season, one can also get some the best strawberries in the country.

Hahndorf is home to many landscape artists and artisans and it is no wonder that there are many souvenir and gift shops where one can pick some unique gifts to make the visit memorable. The Hahndorf Academy - http://www.hahndorfacademy.org.au/ is one such place where local arts and crafts are highlighted and promoted. It also has a museum on German migration and German art.

Although Hahndorf retains an old European charm, it is also recognized as a trendy place for a romantic getaway or a quiet day-off. Many chic restaurants and cafes offer the very best in the world of cuisine.

National Motor Museum

Since its founding in 1965 in Birdwood, the National Motor Museum has greeted millions of enthusiasts with its collection, display and education of Australian transport over the centuries. With over 300 vehicles on display, it is the largest motor museum in Australia.

The collections at the museum range from vintage and classic vehicles to modern vehicles and motorcycles. There is also a section on toys and models.

The museum is open daily (except Dec 25) from 10:00 am to 5:00 pm. Ticket prices are: Adult - $12; and Child - $5. Concession tickets and group discounts are available.

Glenelg

With spectacular sandy beaches, al fresco dining, 200 specialty shops, heritage walks, and a vibrant nightlife, the beach suburb of Glenelg is a popular destination for the locals and tourists alike. Located on the Holdfast Bay shore, Glenelg was founded in 1836, making it the oldest European settlement in the Australian mainland.

Glenelg is conveniently connected to Adelaide by the Anzac Highway. One can use the Adelaide Metro service to reach Glenelg. It is interesting to note that the only tram that operates in the city of Adelaide is the Glenelg Tram - a route that was established in 1873 and is still operational. The highlight is the early 19th century tram that is used on this route on weekends and holidays. Once in Glenelg, most of the attractions can be seen on foot, especially on Jetty Road, the main street that cuts through the middle of the town.

A walk through the streets is nothing short of a heritage walk and one is easily transported back by decades. History lovers can head to the Bay Discovery Centre in the Glenelg Town Hall. The Centre - a museum of social history highlighting the cultural heritage of the region has numerous displays of paintings, sculptures, photographs, jewelry, and other forms of artworks by established as well as rising Australian artists. This self-guided museum is open from 10:00 am to 5:00 pm every day and has free entry.

The Glenelg seafront is packed with activities throughout the week, and gets especially busy on the weekends. Other than just relaxing on the beach, one can engage in many beach activities like scuba diving and beach volleyball. Dolphin watching is also very popular. The multi-award winning Temptation Sailing (Tel: 412 811 838) takes its guests on a 58ft catamaran for a guaranteed full-commentary dolphin cruise. There are a lot of fun activities for families with kids. The Ice Arena, Laser Skirmish, Plaster Fun House, The Fairy Bay Shop, and the Treasure Hunt can keep any kid happy for hours. There is also the refurbished 120-year old carousel, mini golf, and waterslides for the whole family to enjoy.

Glenelg has a very vibrant nightlife with many restaurants, bars, cafes, and nightclubs. There are a wide range of exquisite restaurants for fine dining on Jetty Road, Henley Beach, and Brighton. The Pier Bar, The Grand Bar, Broadway Hotel, and the Jetty Hotel are the popular nightlife spots in town.

Glenelg is also a haven for shopaholics. Harbor Town – about 10 minutes from town – has numerous shopping outlets where one can hunt for great deals. Souvenir stores can be found on Jetty Road, Sussex Street, and the Marina Pier.

McLaren Vale Wine Region

Located about 35 km south of Adelaide and ideal for a day trip, the McLaren Vale Wine Region is regarded as the birthplace of the wine industry of South Australia and is home to some of the oldest grape vines in the world. The region has about 65 boutique-sized wineries with nearly 300 independent grape growers.

The McLaren Vale Wine Region is between the Mt Lofty range of hills and the Gulf of St Vincent beaches. Known for its dry Mediterranean-styled climate, the region was originally used for growing cereal crops. Grape vines were planted in the 1st quarter of the 19th century and the region has been known for the wineries ever since. Different types of wines are produced here but the most popular is the Shiraz. Other major varieties from the region include Cabernet Sauvignon, Grenache, and Chardonnay.

Such is the popularity and influence of wine making in the McLaren Vale Township that many of the roads are named after famous wine making families of the region. There are many interesting wine trails in and around McLaren Vale including the Coast to Vines Rail Trail, Shiraz Trail, and the Kidman Trail. Fresh produce does not begin and end with grape growing in the region. The weekend farmer's market is a great place to buy some of the tastiest cheese and locally harvested olives.

On a sunny day one can also head to the Onkaparinge River to paddle a canoe. The river, the 2nd longest of the island nation, leads into the Onkaparinge National Park which has the Echidna Trail with ruins and heritage-listed huts from the late 19th century. Adventure and nature lovers can also head to the Fleurieu Peninsula to observe the rich wildlife or engage in diving and fishing.

Port Adelaide

Located about 14 km northwest of the Adelaide city centre, Port Adelaide is the main port of the city and a part of the City of Port Adelaide Enfield. Gateway for Adelaide to the rest of the world, Port Adelaide was established in the mid 19th century and has played a major role in the shaping the growth of the city. The area is known as the history precinct for the presence of a number of museums and numerous 19th century pubs and buildings.

Popular historical sites in the Port area include the Port Hotel that was opened in 1838. The British Hotel which opened in 1947 is credited for being the longest continually licensed hotel in the area. The late Victorian-styled Dockside Tavern, The Golden Port Tavern, and the Port Dock Brewery Hotel are all operational for over a 100 years and are tourist attractions for their colonial architectural style and of course, their age. A walk along the docks will also take one past some of the finest and oldest colonial buildings in the country. One can also book a cruise at the Port for dolphin watching. For the fitness enthusiasts, kayaking is an option to explore in the Port area.

The 8 km of clean sand from the North Haven to Sephamore is dotted with many restaurants, cafes, and souvenir stores. The Windsor Gardens and Regency Park are not simply public parks, but hubs for public art and cultural heritage. While the adventure lovers can head for kart racing, rock climbing, or laser skirmish; history lovers can head to one of the many museums in Port Adelaide.

Museums in the Port area include the Enfield Heritage Museum (Regency Park), National Railway Museum (Lipson Street), South Australian Aviation Museum (South Lipson Street), Port Adelaide Maritime Museum (Fletcher Road), and South Australian Maritime Museum (Lipson Street). Art lovers can choose from one of the many galleries in town. Café shops and specialty stores also host exhibitions from time to time. Popular galleries include the Sephamore Angel, Mark Lobert Gallery, and Better World Arts. Many of the regular galleries are located on Lipson Street, Port Road, and Commercial Road.

A popular family event in the Port calendar is the Port Festival (usually in October). With free entry to the museums, food stalls, exhibitions, free guided tours, screenings, artists' market, performances, and fun activities for the whole family, the Port area is transformed into a fun arena for a weekend every year.

Kangaroo Island

The 3rd largest Australian island, Kangaroo Island, is also the largest sand island in the world. With pristine wilderness where one can see pelicans flying across the blue skies or koalas cuddling against the eucalyptus trees, no wonder it is one of the most visited tourist attractions in Australia. Iconic Australian landscape and endemic wildlife of the country make the island a top draw for the tourists.

Kangaroo Island is linked by air and sea from the Australian mainland. Rex Airlines - http://www.rex.com.au/ operates daily flights (approx 30 min) from the Adelaide Airport. Ferry services (45min) are available from Cape Jervis – about a 2 km drive from Adelaide CBD. There are coach connections from Adelaide CBD to the ferry port.

Once on the island, one can enjoy sighting many Australian birds and animals that are protected in a natural environment through many nature reserves and national parks. One of the most popular is the Flinders Chase National Park near the south coast of the island. Home to endangered species like the koala, platypus, fur seals, goannas, and echidnas; the Park is also known for many natural wonders like the Admirals Arch and the iconic Remarkable Rocks.

The island has a number of wildlife attractions and tours including the Hanson Bay Wildlife Sanctuary Tour (includes koala sightings and the famous nocturnal tour), Kangaroo Island Penguin Centre Tour (includes an aquarium visit, penguin colony visit, and feeding the fish and pelicans), and Penneshaw Penguin Centre Tour (nocturnal tour of penguin colony).

The island has many trails and walks for visitors of different fitness levels. Whereas the Ironstone Hill Hike, Fish Cannery Walk, Kingscote Coastal Walk, and Murray Lagoon Walk explore the coast and marine life on the island, the Clifftop Hike, Weirs Cove Hike, and the Cape du Couedic Hike explore the scenic beauty with panoramic views of the island and its surroundings.

Kangaroo Island has a range of accommodations for those who want to stay overnight (especially for the nocturnal tours). There are also many facilities for dining. The island also has great opportunities for shopping, especially lavender products and mosaic-glass artworks.

North Terrace

Running east to west, the North Terrace links the Adelaide CBD to the residential suburbs of the city. A stroll along the North Terrace takes one past a number of public buildings, state offices, and attractions. It is one of the most beautiful and decorated parts of the city.

The National Wine Centre on Hackney Road - http://www.wineaustralia.com.au/ is not only a great place to learn about wine making in this part of the country but also to taste some of the products of the region. One can also enjoy a great meal from the tapas menu of the Cellar Door eatery.

King William Road has the Old Parliament House of South Australia - http://www.parliament.sa.gov.au. The Old Parliament House that took 65 years to complete in 1939 is a grand building with Corinthian columns. Although the original plan had a dome and towers, the final execution was devoid of any extravagance due to financial constraints.

The 1856 Adelaide Railway Station is located near the Morphett Street Bridge. The building also houses the Adelaide Casino in a section that is not used by the railway. This terminal station handles over 40000 passengers every day. The station, which was rebuilt in the mid 1980s, includes some heritage-listed sections.

Kintore Avenue is home to the State Library of South Australia - http://www.slsa.sa.gov.au, the mid 19th century South Australian Museum of Natural History, and the 1881 Art Gallery of South Australia. The avenue is also home to the main campuses of the University of Adelaide and the University of South Australia.

The southern part of the North Terrace also has a number of attractions. The Anglican Holy Trinity Church is the largest Anglican Church in the province of South Australia. It also has the historic Scots Church, and the Christian Scientist Church (Pulteney Street).

Other than some parks and parklands, North Terrace has some shopping centres including the popular Myers House and the Rundle Mall.

St Francis Xavier Cathedral

Affiliated to Roman Catholicism, the St Francis Xavier Cathedral is housed in a Gothic Revival styled building. Although the ground breaking was done in 1856 and the first consecration was done 2 years later, the Cathedral was completed in as late as 1996!

The dominating church building has a 36m high tower and has a length of 56.5m. The statue of St John the Baptist on the north western corner of the church was carved in 1925 in Tuscany. The other end - south west corner - has The Lady Altar carved from Carrara marble with inset panels made from the lapis stone. The western side of the Cathedral has the bronze statues of Jesus and Joseph. The eastern side of the Cathedral has the statue of St Patrick. The southern end - the front façade - of the church has lancet windows with beautiful religious artwork.

The cathedral stays busy with Mass, confessions, funerals, weddings, and many other religious festivals. Not only can one visit the church between 7:30 am and 6:30 pm on any day, one can also book a guided tour at http://www.adelcathparish.org/Ministries/Friends-of-Cathedral.htm.

Belair National Park

Located 13 km south of Adelaide, Belair National Park (Tel: 08 8278 5477) is the place to be for those who are looking for some outdoor activities. Established in 1891, the Park is the oldest national park in the state and the 2nd oldest in the country. The park spans 835ha and has ample opportunities for recreational and social activities set in an outdoor environment. The Park attracts over a quarter million visitors every year.

The region, one of the few biodiversity hotspots in the country, provides an undisturbed environment for wildlife to flourish - both in the form of flora and fauna. Upgraded with picnic spots and other visitor facilities, the Park is a great place to go for a hike, soak in nature, or to enjoy a fun day out with the whole family. The Park has many facilities for playing tennis, weddings, and for group events. Popular trails in the Park include the Wood Duck Dawdle, Valley Loop Walk, Waterfall Hike, and the Lorikeet Loop Walk.

Public transport to the Park is available from the Adelaide CBD. It is open from 8:00 am until sunset every day, except Christmas Day. The Park may remain closed if there are fire predictions or warnings. There are specific rates for entry and using the park facilities, details of which may be found at:
http://www.environment.sa.gov.au/parks/Find_a_Park/Browse_by_region/Adelaide_Hills/Belair_National_Park/Fees.

Migration Museum

82 Kintore Avenue
Adelaide SA
Tel: 08 8207 7580
http://migration.historysa.com.au/

Established in 1986, the unique Migration Museum is involved with the migration and settlement history of the state of South Australia.

The oldest of its kind in the country, the Migration Museum aims at promoting multiculturalism and cultural diversity and addresses the different aspects of ethnicity, gender, class, region, and age. The museum is a great place to discover the identities of various communities and cultures of South Australia.

The museum has a number of permanent and floating exhibitions. The permanent exhibitions include Impact - a pictorial depiction illustrating the impact of migration on the lives and culture of the Aboriginal people. Behind the Wall is a poignant depiction of the lives - and death - of poor and homeless women and children who lived in the Destitute Asylum. 'Strangers in a Strange Land' tells the stories of the immigrants to South Australia in the late 19th century. 'Leaving Britain and Establishing South Australia' is another interesting permanent exhibition that looks into the lives of the British who moved here to establish a British colony. 'Immigration in the Twentieth Century' and 'Into the Twenty First Century' are 2 other permanent exhibitions that not only look into the stories of immigration of the said centuries but also into, how Australia was able to embrace multiculturalism and develop a diverse cultural scene.

Located close to the Rundle Mall, the Museum is open from 10:00 am to 5:00 pm on weekdays and from 1:00 pm to 5:00 pm on weekends and public holidays. It is closed on Christmas Day and Good Friday. Admission is free.

Adelaide Zoo

Frome Road
Adelaide SA 5000
Tel: 08 8267 3255
http://www.zoossa.com.au/adelaide-zoo

Located north of the Adelaide city centre, the Adelaide Zoo is the 2nd oldest zoo in the country and the only one that is a non-profit organization. Spread over 20 acres, the zoo has over 2000 animals from 300 different species. The premise of the zoo itself is of architectural interest and some parts of it are listed as heritage site.

Having opened in 1883, the zoo today is the home to many animals and birds, some endemic to Australia. The zoo enclosure has birds like finches, parrots, and flamingoes. The zoo originally had 10 flamingoes but many of those were killed in a 1915 drought - today only 2 flamingoes over 70 years of age are the prized possession of the zoo. The zoo has animals from different regions. Animals from the Asian region include the Sumatran Tiger, Sacred Kingfisher, Emerald Dove, Giant Panda, Red Panda, and the Mandarin Duck. From the African region there is the African Lion, Cheetah, Ostrich, Giraffe, and Hamadryas Baboon, to name a few. South America is represented by the Brazilian Tapir, Blue and Gold Macaw, Galapagos Tortoise, and the Chilean Flamingo. Of course, there are many Australian birds and animals including the Australian Fur Seal, Red Kangaroo, and Freckled Duck. The zoo arranges a number of encounters (with the birds and animals) and tours for the visiting guests, details of which are posted on the website.

The zoo is open 9:30 am to 5:00 pm everyday and has an entry fee $31.50 for age 15 years and above. Group and family discounts are available.

Recommendations for the Budget Traveller

Places to Stay

Mantra Hindmarsh Square

55 -67 Hindmarsh Square
Adelaide SA 5000
Tel: 08 8412 3333
http://www.mantra.com.au

Located just minutes away from the Adelaide Convention Centre and the Adelaide Cricket Ground in the CBD, the Mantra Hindmarsh Square offers a combination of convenience with style.

Facilities include a 24-hour reception, 24-hr room service, undercover parking (for a fee), travel desk, and laundry facilities. There is free Wi-Fi in the premise. The hotel has a restaurant, lounge bar, and gymnasium.

The apartment-styled rooms come with a kitchenette and some even have a balcony. Room rates start from $129.

Adelaide Royal Coach

24 Dequetteville Terrace
Adelaide SA 5067
Tel: 08 8362 5676
http://www.royalcoach.com.au/

Located close to the business district, the Adelaide Royal Coach is a 3-storey motel with a 90s décor. The National Wine Centre and the East End Precinct are attractions near the motel. There is a 24-hr reception, free parking, and free Wi-Fi. There is a swimming pool, bar, and a restaurant in the premises. Non-smoking rooms and breakfast in the rooms are available.

There are a variety of rooms from the general double rooms to the spa suite. Room rates start from $100.

Adelaide City Park Motel

471 Pulteney Street
Adelaide SA
Tel: 08 8223 1444
http://www.citypark.com.au/

This boutique motel with exquisitely detailed interiors is located at the heart of the city centre, offering a tranquil retreat at affordable rates. Leather lounges and French prints create a warm décor for this motel. This non-smoking property has free parking and Wi-Fi. There is a travel desk and arrangement for airport pick-ups and drops.

Rooms have ensuite bathrooms and tea and coffee facilities. Room rates start from $80 if booked online in advance.

Glenelg Motel

41 Tapleys Hill Road
Glenelg, SA 5045
Tel: 08 8295 7141
http://www.glenelgmotel.com.au

Located just a 5-minute walk from the beach, the Glenelg Motel comes with free parking, free Wi-Fi, and a travel desk. Non-smoking and family rooms are available as well as facilities for disabled guests. There is an outdoor pool and barbeque area. The reception desk closes at 9:00 pm so guests coming after 9:00 pm should notify the motel for late check-in.

Rooms come with ensuite bathroom, LCD TV, tea and coffee facilities, and hairdryer. Room rates start from $110.

The Hotel Metropolitan

46 Grote Street
Adelaide SA 5000
Tel: 08 8231 5471
http://www.hotelmetro.com.au/

The Hotel Metropolitan is housed in a heritage-listed building that was built in 1883.

It is located right at the heart of the city centre adjacent to the Her Majesty's Theatre and the Adelaide Central Markets. The hotel has been functional as a pub from the very beginning and still offers the same, along with games and entertainment. There is free parking and Wi-Fi. Family and non-smoking rooms are available. There is an onsite ATM machine.

Rooms come with a balcony and range from single to multi-person. Room rates start from $55.

Places to Eat

Georges on Waymouth

20 Waymouth Street
Adelaide SA 5000
Tel: 08 8211 6960
http://www.georgesonwaymouth.com.au/

Located in the heart of the Adelaide CBD, the Georges on Waymouth is a multi-award winning restaurant serving Mediterranean cuisine in a European setting. Food is cooked with freshly available produce and the menu for the season is set accordingly. Vegetarian starters are priced about $18. Hand-made pasta is priced between $30-35. Main dishes of pork, beef, or meat are priced between $35 and $40. Dessert wine is offered – priced around $75(circa 2009) for 375ml.

Auge Ristorante

22 Grote Street
Adelaide SA 5000
Tel: 08 8410 9332
http://www.auge.com.au/

As is obvious from the name, this restaurant serves Italian cuisine and is a favorite for business lunches as well as for special occasion dining, at an affordable price. A well-trained attentive staff with excellent service adds to the reputation. Both vegetarian and non-vegetarian entrees are priced at $24. Main dishes of duck, pork, or fish are priced at $39. Italian desserts are priced at $16.50. The restaurant accepts all major credit cards as well as bitcoins.

Taste of Nepal

300 The Parade
Adelaide SA 5068
Tel: 08 8332 2788
http://www.tasteofnepal.com.au/

Serving Nepalese and Indian cuisine, the Taste of Nepal is a favorite with diners, local and visitors alike. If informed earlier, the restaurant makes an effort to cook to accommodate guests with specific food-allergies or any special request.

Entrees (momos and fried vegetables) are priced at $10.50. Main dishes (grilled meat, various non-vegetarian curries) are priced between $20 and $26. Vegan and vegetarian dishes are priced between $17 and $22. It also offers a wide variety of wines.

Jolleys Boathouse Restaurant

1 Jolleys Lane
Adelaide SA 5000
Tel: 08 8223 2891
http://www.jolleysboathouse.com/

Serving international and Australian cuisine, the restaurant serves all the major meals of the day, from breakfast and lunch, to late night dinner. The menu is seasonal depending on the best available produce in the market. Entrees (seafood, chicken, and vegetarian) are priced around $20. Main dishes (of lamb, chicken, and beef) are priced around $35. There is also a huge variety of beer, champagne, and wine to choose from.

Vietnam Restaurant

73 Addison Road
Adelaide SA 5013
Tel: 08 8447 3395
http://www.vietnamrestaurant.com.au/

Established almost 3 decades ago, this is one of the oldest Vietnamese restaurants in Adelaide. This multi award winning restaurant is one of the best places to try Asian cuisine. One can try authentic Vietnamese dishes like the Hot and Sour Fish Soup ($40 – to share), Barbeque quails ($30), Rice paper rolls with stuffing ($4.40), and Crispy king prawns in ginger and chilli ($30). Set menus are also available for groups. Reservations are recommended for this busy restaurant.

Places to Shop

Rundle Mall

Located on Pulteney Street and Rundle Street, the Rundle Mall is the first pedestrian mall in Australia – after traffic was closed on the Rundle Street on September 1976. The mall retains its place as one of the premiere shopping destinations in the city with over a 1000 stores that include many flagship stores along with small independent retailers. It has multiple food courts, bars, and restaurants. The Rundle Mall precinct is also home to over half a dozen places of accommodation! It is a perfect place to not only shop till you drop, but also grab a bite or retire for the day.

North Adelaide Village

http://www.northadelaidevillage.com.au

Located in the famed North Adelaide suburb with numerous restaurants, bars, and shopping centres, the North Adelaide Village is a one stop shopping centre with a variety of stores that include bookstores, salon, jewelry store, optometrist, gym, and a gourmet supermarket. This is the place if someone is looking for cutting edge fashion. The centre also has many restaurants and banks. It is open from 9:00 am to around 5:30 pm with extended hours (9:00pm) on Thursdays.

Adelaide Central Market

Located near the corner of Grote Street, this central market is popular for the fresh produce. This 140 year old market is one of the oldest indoor markets in the world and is a major tourist attraction. It is often called the 'Heart of Adelaide'. Adelaide and its surroundings have a very favourable climate for some Mediterranean-type vegetation and this is the market where one can buy the produce. The market is open from Tuesday to Saturday.

Skye Cellars

578 The Parade
Adelaide SA 5072
Tel: 08 8332 6407
http://www.skyecellars.com.au

Housed in the heritage-listed Auldana Estate Winery, this is a place where one can get some great bargains for the famous South Australian wines. It is 15 minutes from the Adelaide CBD and the ideal place to pick a bottle of wine if one is running a tight schedule and cannot visit the wine region. They have excellently trained staff who may even offer a wine tasting session before recommending a variety.

Gepps Cross Treasure Market

Gepps Cross
Adelaide SA 5094
Tel: 08 8352 1377
http://www.wallis.com.au/gepps-x-market

The biggest outdoor market in the state is also the perfect place to hunt for bargains. From the freshest of fruits and vegetables to the wide variety of antiques and secondhand items, this flea market has something for everyone. It is open every Sunday morning and buyers are allowed from 7:00 am. It is a good idea to get there early to get the best bargains as well as to avoid the crowd.

Darwin & Ayers Rock

Darwin is Australia's gateway to the Asian Far East and also to the sparsely populated Australian Outback. It is a city characterized by a vibrant fusion of east and west, of the youthful and the ancient.

Darwin enjoys beautiful waterfront scenery, thanks to its location along the Timor Sea, while the landscape makes way for timeless desert, monsoon forests and mysterious geographic formations, as you head south towards the heart of Australia.

Ayers Rock (also known by its Aboriginal name of Uluru) and the Kakadu National Park combine natural splendour with mystical significance. Gaze at rock paintings that date back thousands of years and connect with the spirit of the land through an intimate encounter with the Aboriginal culture.

The wildlife of Australia is different from in the other continents. It is home to the kangaroo and the wallaby and the emu, as well as a colorful variety of birdlife and some of the meanest crocodiles to be found anywhere. Crocosaurus Cove offers the rare adrenaline rush of a safe swim with these ancient behemoths. For a unique accommodation option, consider Feathers Sanctuary, a bed and breakfast located within a private bird park. (http://www.audleytravel.com/destinations/australasia /australia/accommodation/feathers-sanctuary.aspx)

Fans of aviation history may find the whole Northern Territory fascinating, as pioneering aviators feature prominently in the region's history. Darwin was, for instance, the only part of Australia that was extensively bombed by the Japanese during World War Two. Both Darwin and Alice Springs have museums dedicated to the history of aviation and Katherine, 300km south of Darwin, also has a few flying legends in its general museum. Equally fascinating, is the story of Australia's unlikely pioneers of long distance travel - the cameleers from Afghanistan.

Expect the unexpected, from this northern tip of the Deep South - and be sure to pack a good camera to document all your adventures in this scenic land.

Culture

Australia has a predominantly Western culture which is strongly influenced by its colonization by Britain. English is the language used by most of its inhabitants and English sport, such as rugby and cricket are also very popular. 68 percent of the Northern Territory's population is European with most hailing from England, Ireland and Scotland.

In Darwin, however, the influence of the Asia is a noticeable factor. Australia has a large Chinese community, which includes people from Mainland China, Hong Kong, Timor and Taiwan. In Australia, facilities such as temples are often shared by different faiths, such as Buddhism and Taoism. The Chinese represent about 4 percent of the Northern Territory's people.

Besides Chinese, Indonesia also exerts some cultural influence on Australia. Indigenous people of Australia have had trade relations with Makassans from Indonesia from the mid 1600s and their trade fostered relationships between different Aboriginal groupings and even gave them a shared language in the form of pidgen Makassan. During the mid to late 19th century, Indonesian workers were brought to Australia and, following Japan's occupation of former Dutch colonies during World War Two, Australia, along with Britain played a role in ousting the Japanese. Today, Indonesian is taught as a non-compulsory second language in Australian schools and the cuisine makes a popular alternative to Chinese and Thai food.

About 40 percent of the Northern Territory is held by Aboriginal land trusts and tribes representing over 40 different language groups are spread throughout the area. They represent one of the world's most ancient living cultures. The concept of Dream Time forms an integral part of the spirituality and social code of all Aboriginal groupings. Tribes are divided into smaller family clans, each of which have their own collection of symbols and sacred sites. Dream Time reflects into the everyday doings of people. It also refers to a dynamic and mythic past when giant super beings roamed the earth, and leaving their imprint on it, through their adventures. The largest Aboriginal communities in the Northern Territory are the Pitjantjatjara near Uluru, the Arrernte around Alice Springs, the Luritja, the Warlpiri and the Yolngu around Arnhem land.

Visitors should bear in mind that a number of alcohol restrictions exists in parts of the Northern Territory. In Alice Springs, Katherine and Tennant Creek alcohol for private use cannot be bought before 2pm and it may not be consumed within 2km of a licensed venue or within remote Aboriginal communities. Restrictions also apply in some sections of Darwin.

Location & Orientation

Darwin is located in the Northern Territory, the central Northern region of Australia. The Northern Territory is bounded to the west by Western Australia, to the east by Queensland and to the south by South Australia. It lies along the Timor sea, 656km from Dili, the capital of East Timor, 1,818km from Port Moresby in Papua New Guinea and 2,700km from Jakarta, the capital of Indonesia.

There are regular flights from Singapore to Darwin and Darwin is also connected by air to various major Australian cities such as Sydney, Perth and Adelaide. A single highway, Stuart Highway, connects Darwin by road to Alice Springs and Adelaide. From Tennant Creek, Barkly Highway connects the Northern Territory to Queensland and from Katherine, Victoria connects to Western Australia. As travel through the Northern Territory involves long distances, travel by rented car or through tour operators may be the best way to cover as much of the region's attractions as possible.

There is also a tourist train, The Ghan (http://www.greatsouthernrail.com.au/site/the_ghan.js p), which connects Darwin to Adelaide, via twice weekly trips, with stops at Katherine, Tennant Creek and Alice Springs. The service has been operational for more than eighty years. Bear in mind, this is a scenic excursion, with the train making a five hour stop in Katherine and a four hour stop in Alice Springs along the way. The travel time runs approximately between 51 and 54 hours.

One of Darwin's most affluent suburbs is the coastal neighbourhood of Larrakeya, which includes the Myilly Point Heritage district, as well as the botanical gardens and the popular Mindil Beach area. Other suburbs are Brinkin, Coconut Grove, Millner and Karama.

Climate & When to Visit

Darwin's weather is characterized by two main seasons of wet and dry weather. The wet season falls in the summer months, which is from December to March, when spells of intense rainfall and periodic storms occur. Floods and cyclones are not unusual during this time, and many attractions are closed or inaccessible due to flooding risk. The rain provides a slightly moderating effect on temperatures, but day temperatures can still average around 32 degrees Celsius with night temperatures typically staying around 25 degrees Celsius. November tends to be the hottest month around Darwin, as it is just before the rainy season begins and day temperatures of around 34 degrees Celsius are usual.

Even in the winter months from June to August, day averages still tend around 31 degrees Celsius, but night temperatures drop to between 19 and 20 degrees Celsius. The autumn months are pleasant and dry. One of the most popular months for tourists is September.

Towards the south, the Northern Territory progressively becomes drier and extreme temperatures can be experienced. For example, at Uluru/Ayers Rock, summer temperatures can go as high 47 degrees Celsius in summer or as low as -7 degrees Celsius in winter. Kakadu National Park experiences a six season cycle. Yegge, from May to June is cool and misty. Wurrgeng, from June to August, is cold and relatively dry. In mid-August, this gives way to Gurrung, a hot, dry spell that lasts till October. From mid-October through to December, humidity builds as the monsoon period becomes eminent. This is known as Gunumeleng. Gudjewg, from January to March is when the monsoon breaks with heavy rains, thunderstorms and flooding. In April, comes Banggereng and the rain clears, although occasional windstorms still occur.

Sightseeing Highlights

Darwin

Darwin is the largest city in the Northern territory and also its capital. Its convenient proximity to Southeast Asia has made a gateway to the East. The city has no direct connection to the famous Charles Darwin, but was named after him by one of his former shipmates from his voyage aboard the *Beagle*.

If you wish to take in the city's beautiful seaside location, stroll along the Darwin Wharf Precinct. On a hot day, you can enjoy a cooling splash or two in the wave pool, which offers swimming safe from Australia's fearsome sea crocodiles. There is a toddler pool and sunbeds, umbrellas, body boards and inflatable rings are available. Admission to this attraction is A$7. You can also relax on a bench, on the grass or seated at one of the area's cafes or restaurants.

Fancy a movie? Take a seat at the Deckchair Cinema (http://www.deckchaircinema.com.au/), an open air theatre located in a tropical garden. It offers beautiful sunset sea views, before you settle down for the film show, which could feature innovative independent festival movies or classics from yesteryear. There are two marine attractions. Indo Pacific Marine, on the Stokes Hill Wharf, seeks to educate visitors about the biodiversity of coral reefs. At Aquascene (http://aquascene.com.au/) on Doctors Gully road, you can experience the rewarding thrill of hand feeding a variety of fish, including butterfly fish, batfish; milkfish, bream, catfish, parrot fish, diamond fish and cod. Admission is A$15.

A somewhat austere historical facility is the Fannie Bay gaol, located along East Point Road, where visitors can view the gallows and the wire enclosed cells, with blocks for males, females and children, as well as two isolated garden cells for the mentally ill. The prison was in use from 1883 to 1979. The Museum & Art Gallery of the Northern Territory at Conacher Street on Bullocky Point, you can view a mixed palette of Darwin's natural and man made heritage.

There is a large variety of Aboriginal art and the remains of a good selection of indigenous fauna. A prize specimen is the body of Sweetheart, a 5.1m seawater crocodile that had been the scourge of boats and other vessels during the mid to late 1970s. There is also an exhibition and video clips to illustrate the devastation wreaked by Cyclone Tracy in 1974. High rollers can try their luck at the Skycity Darwin Casino, while speed junkies can test their skills at racing and drifting at the Hidden Valley Motor Sports Complex.

Apart from its own charms, Darwin offers a great base from which to explore other attractions of the Northern Territory, such as Alice Springs, Ayers Rock or Uluru (as it is now known), Kakadu National Park and the Tiwi Islands, where Aboriginal culture merges with Polynesian influences.

Crocosaurus Cove

Corner of Mitchell & Peel Streets,
Darwin, Northern Territory, Australia
Tel: 61 8 8981 7522
http://www.crocosauruscove.com/

Crocodiles are common in Australia and they feature prominently in legends, popular culture and aboriginal folklore. Their size, appearance and aggression make them seem formidable and dangerous, but in reality, a surprisingly small number of people are harmed crocodiles each year.

You can meet and greet over 70 different reptile species in the reptile enclosure at Crocosaurus Cove, including bearded dragons and snakes. At the turtle sanctuary, you will be able to view a variety of Australian freshwater species, including snapping turtles, red and yellow-faced turtles and pig nosed turtles. As far as the crocodiles go, you will be able to handle a hatchling, assist with feeding juveniles and view a powerful demonstration of the bite force of a fully grown adult.

For adrenaline junkies, the highlight will be a 15 minute session inside the Cage of Death. In this immersive activity, visitors are lowered in a transparent cylindrical cage, to share a crocodile enclosure with its owners, enjoying 360 degree views from up close and personal. Booking may be necessary to avoid disappointment. Another unique experience will be swimming with crocodiles. Professional glossy photographs will be taken of some of the activities and are available for sale. Admission is A$32, but some activities are charged separately.

Other Crocodile Farms

There are other facilities for crocodile watching. The Darwin Crocodile farm (http://www.crocfarm.com.au/) has a population of up to 10,000 crocs and you can enquire about holiday work, if your visa allows it.

There are informative displays to illustrate the life cycle of the crocodile. Crocodylus Park (http://www.crocodyluspark.com.au/) at 815 McMillans Road, Knuckey Lagoon is a small zoo that also houses lions, tigers, emus, kangaroo, wallaby, iguanas, pythons, anacondas, various types of monkeys and turtles. The crocodiles are, of course, the main attraction and the park has several species. There is a crocodile museum, a viewing platform for feeding times and a gift shop selling crocodile related merchandize. You will also have the opportunity to handle baby crocodiles. Admission is A$40. Tours happen at 10am, 12pm and 2pm.

Defence of Darwin Experience

5434 Alec Fong Lim Drive
East Point, Darwin,
Northern Territory 0801, Australia
Tel: 08 8981 9702
http://www.defenceofdarwin.nt.gov.au/

Fans of military history will probably love a visit to the Defence of Darwin Experience, a museum that focuses on Darwin's role in World War Two. It is a little known fact that Darwin had been more heavily bombed than Pearl Harbour. This event is graphically depicted in a series of informative and interactive displays that highlight the events of 19 February 1942.

Video footage features interviews with servicemen based in the North Territory and also documents the war experience from the perspective of different individuals. An outdoor exhibition introduces visitors to the massive guns, tanks, cannons and other assorted military vehicles. Admission is A$14. There is a small gift shop, as well as a cafe that serves snacks.

Australian Aviation Heritage Centre

557 Stuart Highway Winnellie,
Darwin, Northern Territory 0821, Australia
Tel: 8 8947 2145
http://www.darwinsairwar.com.au/

Anyone with even a passing interest in aviation, would be well advised to pay a visit to the Australian Aviation Heritage Centre. Darwin's air facilities played a key role in both civilian and military aviation and some of the legends to pass over Darwin include Amelia Earhart, Amy Johnson, Bert Hinkler and Kingsford Smith, the Australian who made the first trans-Pacific flight. The star exhibit is a huge B52 bomber, on permanent loan from the United States Air Force. Other planes from different eras include a Sabre jet, a mirage, a spitfire and a tiger moth. There are also historical photographs, audio-visual material detailing the Japanese raid of 19 February 1942 and other memorabilia. The gift shop sells books and related souvenirs. Admission is A$14.

Chinese Temple and Museum Chung Wah

25 Woods Street,
Darwin, Northern Territory 0800, Australia
http://www.chungwahnt.asn.au/

The Northern Territory has a large and fairly diverse Chinese community, dating back to the 1870s and it includes people of Hong Kong, mainland China, Timor and Taiwan. The first Chinese temple was built in 1887 and its current temple was built in 1977, following the damage to the previous one by World War Two and Cyclone Tracy. It follows a busy calendar of festivals, since the facility is shared by Buddhists, Taoists and followers of Confucius. The entrance is guarded by stone lions crafted in China and a sacred Bodhi tree, said to be a descendant of the one under which Buddha sat when he attained enlightenment, grows on the grounds. The museum is manned by volunteers and has limited hours. Do act respectfully when visiting the temple. Do not touch any of the objects on the altar and avoid photographing visitors.

Pudakul Aboriginal Cultural Tours

Arnhem Highway, Adelaide River,
Darwin, Northern Territory, Australia
Tel: 61 0 8984 9282
http://www.pudakul.com.au/

The Pudakul Aboriginal Cultural experience introduces visitors to a wealth of information regarding wildlife, native plants, spirituality and aboriginal family life. There are demonstrations to educate about indigenous weaving techniques, spear throwing, clay sticks and playing the didgeridoo. Local food and bush medicine is also covered in the presentation. There are daily two hour tours starting at 10.30am from April through to November. The cost is A$49 per person.

Kakadu National Park

Kakadu National Park is at 110,000 square km the largest national park in Australia and it also contains some of the best examples of Aboriginal rock art. The art at Nourlangie's Anbangbang gallery is well known and includes work as recent as 1964, added by Nayombolmi, of the Badmardi clan. It features the mythical characters of Namarrgon, Namondjok and Barrginj.

To the west, is Nangawulurr Shelter, a refuge used by the Warramal clan and another Aboriginal gallery. There is also rock art at the Ubirr site and movie fans may recognize this as one of the locations in the Crocodile Dundee film. A popular route near Ubirr is the Bardedjilidji Walk, but do check in at the Bowali Visitor Centre beforehand, as the staff there will be able to organize guides and advise you, if there is any flooding hazard. More challenging walks include the 3.6km Mirrai Lookout Walk and the 12km Barrk Sandstone Walk, which passes features like Nourlangie Rock and Nanguluwur Art Gallery.

Besides the rock art, you may also see plenty of wildlife, such as wallabies, frilled lizards and even groups of feral pigs, water buffalo and horses. There are fascinating termite mounds, rugged mountains and colonies of wetland birds, like the enigmatic 'Jesus' bird that cruises from lily pad to lily pad, ospreys, sea eagles, magpie geese, egrets and herons. A great place for watching the wildlife is the Yellow Water Billabong, a placid estuary of the East Alligator River.

At the southern end of Kakadu, you can see the dramatic sight of the 200m Jim Jim (http://www.jimjimfalls.com/) Falls and Twin Falls. That is, unless you visit in the dry season between July and October, when it becomes a barren gorge. If you dare, do book a crocodile spotting river cruise. A great place to relax and picnic is the Gunlom Plunge Pool. Whatever you plan to do at Kakadu National Park, do bring lots of bottled water as temperatures can exceed 40 degrees Celsius.

Warradjan Cultural Centre

Kakadu Highway, Jim Jim,
Kakadu National Park,
Northern Territory 0886, Australia
Tel: +61 8 8979 0145
http://www.gagudju-dreaming.com/Indigenous-
Experience/Warradjan-Cultural-Centre.aspx

The Warradjan Cultural Centre shares informative material on the region's geography, history and indigenous fauna and flora. Some of the subjects covered include mythology, celestial events and various rites of passage. There is also a gift shop that sells a large selection of Aboriginal art, including bark paintings, as well as books, traditional music and T-shirts. The Warradjan Cultural Centre is air-conditioned and admission is free.

Tiwi Islands

The Tiwi Islands are located about 80km north of Darwin, roughly where the Arafura Sea merges with the Timor Sea. The largest islands are Melville and Bathurst, but there are also nine uninhabited islands. The islands have a combined population of about 3000, of which 90 percent are Aboriginal, but they are believed to have been occupied for around 7000 years. The culture of the islands represent an interesting blend of Aboriginal and Polynesian cultures.

Visitors will need a permit for the islands and there are practically no facilities for tourists. Adventurous visitors may wish to participate in a deep-sea fishing expeditions. Distinctive to the island are elaborately decorated "pukamanis" or burial poles that can be as high as 3m. Most of the carvings depict birds, which are integral to the island's mythology. The Tiwi Islands can be reached by light aircraft from Darwin. There is also a ferry service between Darwin and Bathurst Island. Unique craft items items can be bought on the islands.

Litchfield National Park

http://www.litchfieldnationalpark.com/

Litchfield National Park is located about 100km southwest of Darwin and was named after Frederick Henry Litchfield, one of the first European explorers of the northern end of Australia. The park contains some of the region's best examples of magnetic termite mounds, which can be accessed via a route of boardwalks.

Other features include the Bamboo Creek tin mine, several waterfalls such as Wangi Falls, Tjaynera Falls, Surprise Creek Falls and Florence Falls and Blyth Homestead, which was built in 1929. Some of the indigenous wildlife includes kangaroo, wallaby, possums, flying foxes, dingo and ghost bats, as well as a large variety of bird species such as the black kite, yellow oriole, figbird and rainbow bee-eater. The park is home to isolated sections of monsoon rainforest, but also has lovely ground orchids. There are various camping and caravan sites.

Alice Springs

Alice Springs is located right at the heart of Australia. It is just under 1500km from Darwin to the north and about 1500km from Adelaide to the south. If you want the remoteness of the Outback to hit home, visit two unique facilities created to bridge some of the large distances of the region. Both the School of the Air and the Royal Flying Doctors Service are headquartered in Alice Springs.

The School of the Air is located at 80 Head Street and provides a glimpse into some of the challenges faced by educators in order to bring schooling to students on remote ranches, some as far as 1500km away. Initially a radio service, the School of the Air now utilizes computers and satellite communication. Also based in Alice Springs is the visitors centre of the Royal Flying Doctors Service (http://www.rfdsalicesprings.com.au/). This life saving service, founded by John Flynn in 1928, operates from 21 bases and promises to be able to reach any patient within the coverage area in two hours. At the Visitors Centre, you can watch an informative video and also see some of the early equipment used. Then, compare that to the modern technology of today, which can track any plane in the service in real time. Finally, take a good look inside a replica of one of the specially adapted planes. Admission is A$12, with an optional A$2 to see the inside of the plane. A gift shop sells branded merchandize.

In Alice Springs, the Great Outdoors is huge, and instantly accessible. Animal lovers will probably enjoy a visit to the Kangaroo Sanctuary (https://www.kangaroosanctuary.com/). Here they can meet kangaroo rescuer, Brolga, featured as *Kangaroo Dundee* on BBC2 and his charges, which includes the enormous male, Roger. Booking is essential. A sunset tour costs A$85. The Alice Springs Reptile Centre is located opposite the Flying Doctor's Visitors Centre. There are around 30 different species such as bearded dragons, pythons, iguana, blue tongued lizards, gecko, crocodiles and sand goanna and visitors will have the opportunity to handle some of these. Admission is A$13.

Car enthusiasts should consider a visit to the Road Transport Hall of Fame (http://www.roadtransporthall.com/), where they can meet some of the mechanical workhorses of the past. The National Pioneer Women's Hall (http://www.pioneerwomen.com.au/) showcases the achievements of various women who were pioneers of their field. A prize exhibit is a quilt featuring the signatures of most of the women included in the display. The Alice Springs Telegraph Station Reserve once served as an important link in the chain of communication between Adelaide and Darwin. Established in 1873, it was operational for almost six decades and was later utilized as a school for Aboriginal children. It is located along South Stuart Highway.

For a good overview of what Alice Springs has to offer, why not book a ride aboard the hop-on-hop-off town tour (http://www.alicewanderer.com.au/12-alice-explorer-hop-hop-off-town-tour.html), which stops at various of the town's attractions such as the Old Telegraph Station, Anzac Hill, the Royal Flying Doctor Base, Reptile Centre, Olive Pink Botanical Garden and Todd Mall. A ticket costs A$44.

Camel Tours

Camels once played an integral role in creating the infrastructure of Australia's remotest regions. Cameleers from Afghanistan, who arrived down south from the 1860s, were the pioneers of long distance land travel in the Australian outback. For decades, they delivered mail and supplies and when railways and highways were constructed, they provided labour as well as the back-up of transporting vital provisions. Historically, the area was also policed on camelback, a tradition that disappeared in the 1950s.

Today, visitors can explore the region through a camel tour. Camel Tracks (http://www.cameltracks.com/) offers the choice of an hour-long excursion for A$60 or a half day tour for A$110. The experience can also be customized and camel related souvenirs and collectables are available.

Larapinta Trail

A prominent feature of Central Australia is the MacDonnell mountain range. Here, serious hikers would be presented with the challenge of the Larapinta Trail, a 223km route that leads from Alice Springs to Mount Sonder, which is, at 1380m, one of the highest mountains in the West MacDonnell mountain range after Mount Zeil.

The route has a number of fascinating geographical landmarks, including Brinkley's Bluff, Glen Helen Gorge, Counts Point, Standley Chasm, Ellery Creek Waterhole, Serpentine Gorge and Ormiston Gorge and the Ochre Pits a multi-coloured, layered rock used for Aboriginal Ceremonies. Hikers are strongly advised to schedule their trips for the winter months, from June to August, as summer temperatures in the area can reach around 45 degrees Celsius, creating the risk of heatstroke and dehydration.

Alice Springs Desert Park

Larapinta Drive,
Alice Springs,
Northern Territory 0871, Australia
Tel: +61 8 8951 8788
http://www.alicespringsdesertpark.com.au/

The Alice Springs Desert Park introduces visitors to the
natural fauna and flora of a desert environment.
Highlights of the park's attractions are the bird show,
which displays the skills of its raptors and the guided
nocturnal tour. Admission is A$25. The park has a
program that offers students the opportunity to volunteer
in various fields such as animal keeping and horticulture.

Ayers Rock (Uluru)

http://www.uluru.com/

The enigmatic Ayers Rock, or Uluru, to use its aboriginal
name, is a massive sandstone structure located in the
middle of the Australian Outback, about 450 km from
Alice Springs and what you see, is the just a fraction. The
largest part of the rock is subterranean and extends 2.5km
below the ground. The Aboriginal people believe that the
underground portion of Uluru is hollow and taps into a
powerful well of energy and life force, which they refer to
as Tjukurpa and also the Dreamtime. It functions as a
connection to the ancestors, as well as some type of
Akashic record.

The rock was discovered by the surveyor William Gosse in 1873 and named after Sir Henry Ayers, the Chief Secretary of South Australia at the time. One unique feature is the way the colour of the light changes, as the angle of the sun does, so that the rock appears in different hues at different times of the day. Its orange-red colour is the result of surface oxidation of the iron component of the rock. The rock formation is believed to contain 25 to 35% quartz. Uluru is 3.6km long and 1.9km wide, rising 348m above the plain, but its true height is 860m above sea level. Some of Uluru's caves feature rock art dating back 5000 years.

Uluru/Ayers Rock is listed twice as a World Heritage site - initially in 1987 for its distinctive geographical features and subsequently, in 1997, for its cultural significance to the aboriginal people of Australia. It is regarded as a holy site by the Anangu people, who have lived in the area for approximately 10,000 years. Uluru itself is estimated to be around 600 million years old. It is classified as an inselberg, a term used to describe an "island mountain." Hard to believe now, but this structure began its existence as compressed sediment at the bottom of an ocean.

A trip to Uluru/Ayers Rock can be combined with a cultural experience that will introduce visitors to the indigenous plant and animal life of the region, educate them about bush food and share folk tales and myths about the state of being the Aboriginals refer to as Dream Time. Various types of guided tours are available. Among these options, you can choose from Harley-Davidson tours, Sunrise tours, Sunset tours, stargazing tours, helicopter tours and camel excursions.

A 10.6km looped walk around the base of Uluru will impress you with its size and introduce you to its geographical diversity, as well as its indigenous animal and plant life. At the Cultural Centre, you can learn more about the Rock, buy snacks, arts, crafts and souvenirs from the locals and even enjoy a BBQ. A visit to Uluru is often combined with a trip to Kata Tjuta. Uluru is visited by around 250,000 visitors each year.

Kata Tjuta is located within the same National Park as Uluru. Its highest peak, at 1,066m above sea level, is Mount Olga, which was named after Queen Olga of Württemberg. In the 1950s, the area was made into a National Park, disregarding indigenous claims to the land. In the 1980s, the sites were finally restored to the ownership of Anangu people. There is an agreement of joint management between the Anangu and Australian Parks.

Katherine

Katherine, the third largest settlement in the Northern Territory, is located along the banks of the Katherine river. The river also flows through Katherine Gorge, which is in turn one of the most striking features of the Nitmiluk National Park. The park is 30km from Katherine and also features a scenic but challenging bush-walking route, Jatbula trail, which passes impressive waterfalls as well as the Jawoyn Aboriginal rock art site.

About 30km from Katherine along the Stuart Highway, you will find the Cutta Cutta Caves, a network of limestone caves with interesting Karst features. Mataranka, a small township 107km from Katherine, has hot springs and is associated with a well known Australian novel, *We of the Never Never* by Jeannie Gunn. Popular activities of the region around Katherine include bushwalking, canoeing and helicopter tours. Bear in mind that there is a significant flooding risk during the wet season at most of Katherine's attractions.

Katherine Museum

Gorge Rd

One of the more unusual exhibits at Katherine Museum is a planetarium hand made by one of the area's more eccentric residents, a Russian peanut farmer known as Galloping Jack. There are also various collections of historical photographs, ancient Aboriginal artifacts and relics from World War Two. Admission is A$10.

Recommendations for the Budget Traveller

Places to Stay

Paravista Motel

5 Mackillop Street, Parap,
Darwin, Northern Territory 0820, Australia
Tel: +61 8 8981 9200
http://paravistamotel.com.au/

Located in a quiet street in the Parap Village suburb of Darwin, the Paravista motel has a retro 1970s atmosphere and is conveniently near a number of great shopping opportunities.

The motel has a pool and spa, communal kitchen and BBQ area, laundry and tours can be booked through the Tours desk. Free parking is available. Rooms include air-conditioning, a private bathroom, fridge, television, coffee and tea making facilities and free Wi-Fi internet. Accommodation is charged from A$89 during the wet season and A$129 during the dry season. Larger groups may wish to consider renting a three bed room house at between A$250 and A$325.

Palms Motel

100 McMinn Street,
Darwin, Northern Territory 0800, Australia
Tel: +61 8 8981 4188

Palms Motel is located a short drive from the city centre and a 10 minute walk from the botanical gardens. The motel has an outdoor pool and BBQ facilities. There is also free parking, a DIY laundry service and vending machines. Each room includes en suite bathroom and a kitchenette with microwave, fridge and tea and coffee making facilities. Accommodation begins at A$118. Internet coverage is not available.

Ashton Lodge

48 Mitchell Street,
Darwin, Northern Territory 0800, Australia

Centrally located in Mitchell Street above the Wisdom
Bar, Ashton Lodge is somewhere between a motel and a
backpackers lodge. There is a swimming pool, terrace,
bar, laundry facilities and a communal kitchen, and
guests also qualify for a 10 percent discount at the
Wisdom Bar. Bear in mind, though, that this vibrant
setting can get a little noisy at night. Rooms are basic, but
clean and well-maintained. Wi-Fi coverage is available,
but charged separately. Accommodation begins at A$110.

Value Inn

50 Mitchell Street,
Darwin, Northern Territory 0801, Australia
Tel: +61 8 8981 4733
http://www.valueinn.com.au/

The Value Inn is centrally located in the lively Mitchell
street. There is a swimming pool with pool bar, a
dedicated BBQ area, a waterfall spa, self-catering kitchen,
laundry facilities and an internet cafe. Reception is
available round the clock. All rooms include en suite
bathroom facilities, TV, a bar fridge and tea and coffee
making facilities. Accommodation begins at A$135.

Dingo Moon Lodge

88 Mitchell Street,
Darwin, Northern Territory 0800, Australia
http://www.dingomoonlodge.com/

Since accommodation in Darwin can be quite pricey, you may seriously consider sacrificing a few creature comforts for the cheaper options at hostels or backpackers accommodation. Mitchell Street is a very good place to start looking for some of those. Dingo Moon Lodge is located a little way off from the main nightspots and offers very friendly service. There is also the added bonus of free laundry and a free breakfast. The communal kitchen can get somewhat crowded and rooms are small and basic. Wi-Fi internet coverage is available. Accommodation ranges from dorms for eight, six and four, to double rooms shared between two, with rates from A$24.00 for the most basic dorm bed to A$102.50 per room, for two.

Places to Eat & Drink

The Deck Bar Restaurant

22 Mitchell Street,
Darwin, Northern Territory, Australia
Tel: +61 8 8942 3001
http://www.thedeckbar.com.au/

The Deck Bar restaurant combines friendly service and a great atmosphere with meals at reasonable prices. There is indoor and outdoor seating and a selection of around 80 beers and numerous creative cocktails. The menu is varied and includes regular favourites such as pizza, salads, burgers and grills, as well as a large selection of Asian style dishes such as laksa, pad thai and curry. If you're interested in nibbling and sharing, try one of the platters, priced between A$25 and A$45, which includes different combinations of snacks such as spring rolls, chicken wings, skewers, fries and rice paper rolls.

Alternately, tapas style snacks can be ordered and these include lamb cutlets, dumplings, duck pancakes and spicy salt squids. If you love burgers, try the Double Decker for A$19.90, which is served with fries and salads. Dinner mains are priced between A$14.50 and A$29. Breakfast and brunch options are priced between A$9.50 and A$16. The Deck Bar restaurant also features live or DJ entertainment.

Speaker's Corner Cafe Restaurant

Mitchell Street, Parliament House,
Darwin, Northern Territory, Australia
Tel: 08 8946 1439
http://www.karensheldoncatering.com/speakers_corner
_cafe

For a wholesome breakfast to start your day or a light, but
filling lunch, take a seat at Speaker's Corner Cafe. Some of
the fare will be reminiscent of England. There is a great
selection of sausage rolls and pies such as cornish, beef
and mushroom, creamy chicken or chunky lamb, all
priced at between A$5 and A$8. Fish and Chips will set
you back around A$18 and expect to pay A$16 for a
Classic Aussie burger with chips. Be sure to check out
daily specials such as the roast of the day or the quiche of
the day. Speaker's Corner Cafe also serves slices of cake,
freshly squeezed juices, smoothies, milkshakes, muesli
and toast. The restaurant is open between 7.30am and
4pm.

Sari Rasa Restaurant

6/24 Cavenagh Street,
Darwin, Northern Territory 0800, Australia
Tel: +61 8 8941 9980

Sari Rasa is a small cafe that offers authentic Indonesian
cuisine at budget prices.

Some of the favourites include beef redang, chilli beans and eggplant and dried beef with crispy potatoes. There is a good selection of curries, such as beef, chicken, lamb and fish curry. A large portion costs A$12 and includes the choice of three mains and rice.

Kakadu Bakery Restaurant

Gregory Pl, Jabiru,
Kakadu National Park, Northern Territory, Australia
Tel: 8979 2320

At the Kakadu Bakery you can buy a variety of snacks, treats and light meals on your way to or from the National Park. Service is quick and efficient. Some of the choices include freshly prepared salad, quiches, pizza slices, sandwiches, burgers, cakes and pastries. At between A$4.50 and A$5, the pies are a popular choice and some of the fillings include crocodile, kangaroo meat, buffalo and mushroom.

Page 27 Cafe Restaurant

3 Fan Arcade,
Alice Springs, Northern Territory, Australia
Tel: 08 8952 0191

Located at the end of Todd Mall, Page 27 is a 60s style cafe with great ambiance that serves breakfast and lunch. There are salads, omelettes, cakes, smoothies, muffins and corn fritters, as well as pies and pita wraps. Expect meals between A$8 and A$16.

Places to Shop

Parap Shopping Village

Parap Road, Parap Village Shopping Precinct,
Darwin, Northern Territory 0820, Australia
http://parapvillage.com.au/

There are several shops of interest at Parap Shopping
Village. Nomad Art sells indigenous craft items sourced
from various Aboriginal Art Centres. The Good Luck
Shop (http://www.goodluckshop.com.au/) sells a large
selection of gifts and wellness products, including
incense, wind chimes, essential oils, aromatic candles,
grass woven baskets, jewellery, Egyptian perfume and
other novelty items. Goods include crafted items from
Swaziland, Tibet, Zimbabwe, India, the Philippines and
Vietnam. Outstation showcases the work of established
and upcoming indigenous artists and items include wall
hangings, paintings, woven handbags and toys. Another
gallery selling the work of Aboriginal artists is the Tiwi
Art Network, which specifically focuses on the work of
artists from the Tiwi Islands. For gifts and novelty items,
check out the wares at Paraphernalia. Parap Village also
has various salons, spas, restaurants and other shops.

Besides regular trade, Parap Village is home to one of
Darwin's longest running markets. The market trades
every Saturday from 8am to 2pm and features a large
selection of arts and crafts, clothing, jewellery, handmade
soaps, musical instruments, decor items and skin care
products.

Choose from Vietnamese silk scarves, sarongs, pearls and many more. Besides crafts, there is also a great choice in local fresh produce, flowers, herbs and spices and ready made food. You can snack on Nutella crepes, rice paper rolls, papaya salad and various Asian favourites.

Mindil Beach Markets

Darwin,
Northern Territory, Australia
http://www.mindil.com.au/

Enjoy the beach setting, the beautiful sunset and the live entertainment, which ranges from fire breathers and jugglers to didgeridoo players at Mindil Beach Market. The market has around 60 food stalls, which sell juices, smoothies, ice cream, fruit salad, muffins, burgers, hot dogs, kebabs, sushi, pizza, pasta, BBQ seafood and even crocodile fillets. You can choose from Chinese, Thai, Indian, Mexican, Greek and Sri Lankan food.

The other stalls feature a diverse selection, which includes gems, fabrics, collectible coins, art, handmade puzzles, books, didgeridoos, toys, T-shirts and jewellery from around well over 100 local crafters. There is also a wellness section where you can indulge yourself with a Thai massage, a Chinese massage or a foot massage, consult a tarot reader or try some of the local skin care products or natural bush remedies. Do bear in mind that the venue has no facilities for credit card transactions.

Casuarina Square

Trower Road, Darwin
http://www.casuarinasquare.com.au/

The largest shopping mall in the Northern Territory is Casuarina Square, which is located in the northern suburbs of Darwin. Most major stores have outlets here, and there is also a number of speciality shops. There are two supermarkets, Coles and Woolworths, as well as Kmart, Just Jeans and Priceline. Dollars and Sense (http://www.dollarsense.com.au/) stocks a large variety of items including toys, clothing, home ware, gifts and craft items. Visit Smiggle (http://www.smiggle.com.au/shop/en/smiggle/) for colorful novelty items such as lava lamps, bracelet kits, card making kits, a selection of puzzles and a colour changing brolly (umbrella). J & V Gifts 'n' Novelty (http://www.jvgiftsnnovelty.com/) stocks plush toys, merchandize related to popular anime and computer games, figurines and other toys.

di CROCO

Shop 4, The Vic Complex
27 The Mall, Darwin NT 0800 Australia
Tel: +61 8 8941 4470
http://www.dicroco.com/

Crocodiles are synonymous with Australia.

Therefore it should not come as too much of a surprise that the country has some great outlets for crocodile hide products. Most crocodile farms you visit should have a gift shop that stocks crocodile related products, but for a great range of crocodile hide products, do browse through the wares at di CROCO. You will be able to choose from belts, handbags of various sizes, wallets, purses, pouches, business and travel accessories and also jewellery such as bangles, bracelets, beads, rings, earrings, studs and cufflinks.

Shopping in Alice Springs

At the Todd Mall market, held Sundays from May to December, you can expect plenty of crafts, jewellery and Aboriginal art, as well as an entertaining crew of entertaining buskers. For a great selection of indigenous art, visit Aboriginal Art World (http://www.aboriginalartworld.com.au/), which showcases the work of over 70 artists from South Australia and the desert interior of the Northern territory. Pitjantjatjara is particularly well represented. Other galleries include Mbantua Gallery (http://www.mbantua.com.au), Papunya Tula Artists (http://www.papunyatula.com.au), an Aboriginal owned enterprise representing 120 artists and Ngurratjuta Iltja Ntjarra (http://www.ngurart.com.au). Tjanpi Desert Weavers (http://www.tjanpi.com.au/) is a non-profit organization selling woven baskets and also grass sculptures, such as their desert dogs. Looking for a shopping mall in Alice? Try Yeperenye Shopping Centre (http://www.yeperenye.com.au/). For a selection of personalized gifts, go to Alice Springs Creative Gifts & Awards at 81 Smith Street. Booklovers should check out Dymocks in Alice Plaza, Red Kangaroo Books at 79 Todd Mall or, if they don't mind buying second hand, Bookmark it, at 113 Todd Street.

7709691R00046

Printed in Great Britain
by Amazon.co.uk, Ltd.,
Marston Gate.